Predominant artwork & imagery source:
Shutterstock.com
Copyright: North Parade Publishing Ltd.
4 North Parade,
Bath,
BA1 1LF, UK

First Published: 2019

All rights reserved. No part of this publication may be reprinted, stored in a retrieval system or transmitted, in any form or by any means, electronic, mechanical, photocopying, recording, or otherwise, without the prior permission of the copyright holder.

Printed in China.

Global Warming and Climate Change

CONTENTS

Treasure Trove	6
Increasing Numbers	8
Food to Eat	10
Where are all the Fish?	12
Food for Us?	14
Where's the Water?	16
Air Polution	18
Burning Earth	20
Ozone Hole	22
Rubbish Heap	24
Red Alert	26
Wild Weather	28
Rising Sea Levels	30
Food Shortage	32
At the Poles	34
Change is not Good	36
Human World	38
Spread of Diseases	40
Can We Stop It?	42
You Can Help Too!	44

Treasure Trove

Natural resources are incredibly valuable. They include air, water, sunlight, land, plants and animals and surround all of us every day.

Resources are Important to us

Life on earth depends on natural resources. So, a resource is something that is useful to us. The more natural resources a country has, the richer it is likely to be. Resources can be classified as renewable and non-renewable.

Rainforests are treasure troves of natural resources

ECO fact

Renewable resources have to be given time to renew themselves. Rainforests are being cut down so fast, experts fear they will disappear. Using resources carefully is called sustainable use.

GLOBAL WARMING AND CLIMATE CHANGE

Renewable Resources

Anything that can be made again is a renewable resource. Most renewable resources are living things such as animals, insects, trees and plants. But not all are living things. Sunlight, wind and tides are called 'flow' renewable resources, because they are continuous. Although water is a renewable resource only 3% of the total water on earth is usable. The rest is either frozen or too salty to use.

Non-Renewable Resources

Anything that takes a long time to be made again is a non-renewable natural resource. Coal and oil are non-renewable resources. That is because it takes millions of years for coal and oil to form. Other non-renewable natural resources include: natural gas; minerals such as diamonds; metals like iron ore, copper, gold and silver. The amount of a resource that is available, the time it takes to be made, and its use to us, decides the value or the price of the natural resource.

Coal is one of the most commonly used non-renewable natural resources

Renewable resources like wind are now being used to produce electricity

Increasing Numbers

A collection of people living in a certain place is known as population. The total number of people on earth is called world population.

Growing, Growing, Groan!

Counting the population of a place is called a census. The earliest known census was in Babylon in 3800 BC. The oldest census we can still find records for was taken in 2 AD in China during the Han dynasty. In 1 AD, there were an estimated 200,000 people in the world. By 1804, it was 1 billion. By 1961, it was 3 billion. It took just 13 years to increase that to 4 billion. In 2007, there were over 6.6 billion people on earth. It is projected that by 2011 there will be seven billion people living on this planet!

China has the largest population in the world – over 1.3 billion people!

GLOBAL WARMING AND CLIMATE CHANGE

Increasing population has led to more crowded towns and cities

The Biggest Growth

The last 100 years have seen a rapid increase in population. Medicines and healthcare have improved and lengthened lifespan. Better agriculture means many people have enough to eat. Communications and travel have also improved.

Continent Count

Asia is home to around 3.8 billion people. Africa has about 840 million people. The Americas have around 885 million. Europe comes next with 710 million people and Australia has 21 million. China is the most populated country with 1.32 billion people. India has 1.12 billion and the United States of America comes third with 300 million people.

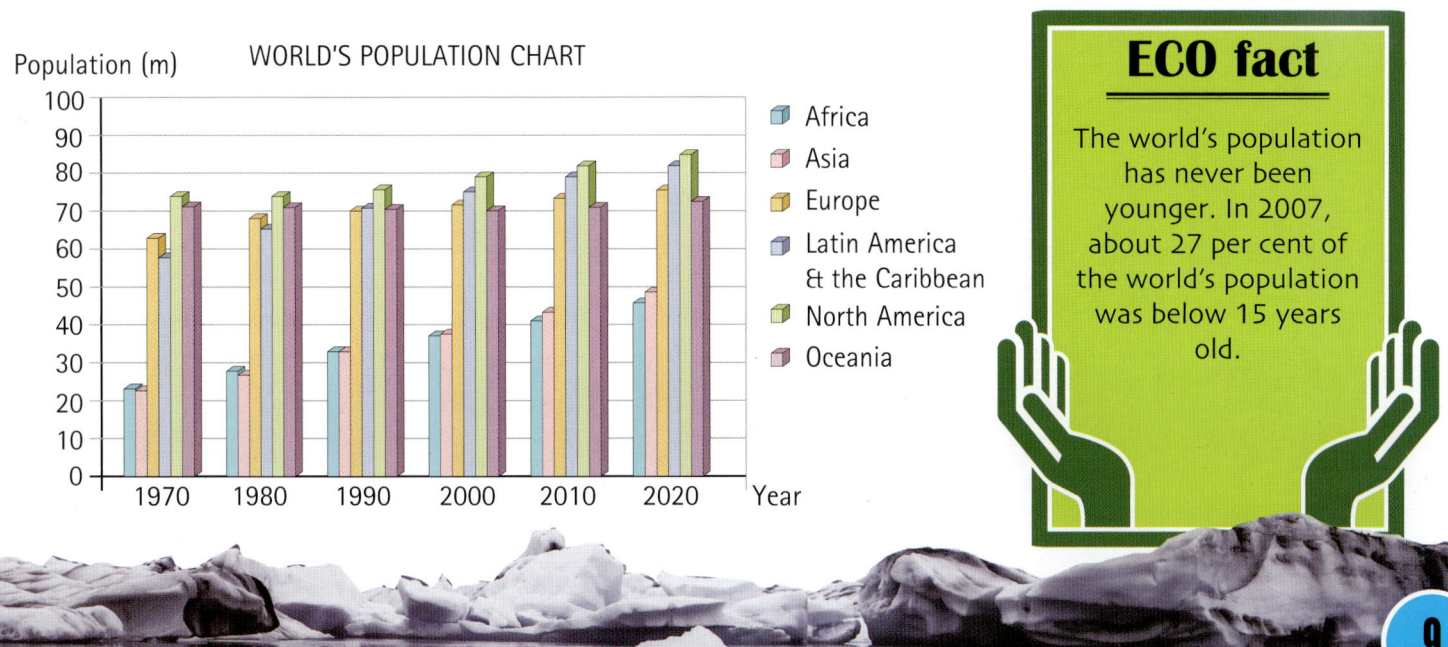

ECO fact

The world's population has never been younger. In 2007, about 27 per cent of the world's population was below 15 years old.

Food to Eat

As the population grows, we need more food to feed the millions, requiring more farmland and water for irrigation.

Give Me More!

Most of our food comes from the land. Grain needs land to grow on and animals need land to graze on. From the time early hunter-gatherers settled down and turned to agriculture, forest cover has been reducing. Most of this loss has been in the past two centuries as populations grew and we cleared forests for farmland. 40 per cent of the land on earth has been brought under agriculture and grazing cattle by human beings.

 Over-grazing has left many places in Africa barren and vulnerable to drought

Not Enough Land

Land for crops is reducing for several reasons. Trees help to break the wind. When you cut trees down, the topsoil is swept away. This happened at Karamay Agricultural Development Region in Xinjiang, China. In some places, the fertile topsoil has been washed away by rain and floods. The overuse of chemical fertilizers can also make soil infertile. Huge hydroelectric projects are taking away acres of farmland. Moreover, many farmers are not aware of the dangers of pumping too much water onto land, making it infertile.

Trees are being cut to make way for farm land

GLOBAL WARMING AND CLIMATE CHANGE

Let's Look Further

With the growing need for food we continue to look for more and more agricultural land. Forests are cleared to provide people with more land to grow crops on. About sixty per cent of the trees cut are to make way for agricultural fields. Thousands of different plant and animal species thrive in forests, enriching ecological diversity. Every time a forest is cleared it takes away the natural habitats of these plants and animals. Instead of concentrating on making more land available for agriculture, it is perhaps more important to improve the quality of land that is available to us. That way we will not need more land.

Over-ploughing can strip soil of its fertility and can cause the loss of valuable topsoil

ECO fact

One out of every three apples grown in the UK lands in the rubbish bin. The amount of food wasted in the country has been rising by 15 per cent every 10 years.

Where are all the Fish?

Overfishing threatens about a third of the world's species of fish, with numbers reduced to below 10 per cent of previously recorded populations.

Modern trawlers use large nets to comb the bottom of the sea, damaging all in their path

Something Fishy

In 1950 about 18m tonnes of fish was landed. By 1969 this had increased to 56m tonnes. However, the population of fish did not grow proportionately. The coastal anchovy fisheries of Peru, for example, produced 10.2m metric tonnes in 1971. The next year, the stocks were down to less than 1m metric tonnes. In 1992, overfishing led Canada to stop fishing on the Grand Banks.

Growing Unlike A Whale

The hunting of whales is banned by many countries. Dspite this, today five out of thirteen great whale species, including the massive blue whale, are endangered due to commercial whaling. During the 19th and 20th centuries whales were widely hunted for their meat and oil. Even today whale oil is in demand, prompting some countries to continue to whale.

GLOBAL WARMING AND CLIMATE CHANGE

In the Soup

The next time you are tempted to order a bowl of shark fin soup, remind yourself that many fins are cut from living sharks, who are then thrown back into the sea to die. The IUCN red list says 39 species of sharks and rays are threatened. In just the last 50 years, the numbers of some shark species have fallen by 50 per cent. The basking shark, the whale shark and the great white shark are threatened species.

ECO fact

It is thought that as much as 70 per cent of fish sold as the highly prized red snapper is in fact another species! This is a phenomenon known as 'species substitution'.

Shark fin soup is a delicacy in countries like China

Whale bones are highly prized in some remote Arctic regions

Food For Us?

In 1998, nearly 280 biologists told the American Museum of Natural History that several species of animals will be wiped out because of human activity.

Mammoths were hunted into extinction by early man

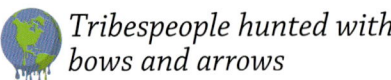

Tribespeople hunted with bows and arrows

Killing Them Off

Since 1500 BC, about 784 species have become extinct. Humans are the biggest threat to other forms of life. Our activities kill other species in several ways: factories release poisonous gases that pollute the atmosphere and untreated waste matter that pollutes lakes, rivers and seas, killing creatures that live there; irresponsible hunting has led to many species becoming extinct; every time a forest is cleared, we lose mammals, birds and insects.

GLOBAL WARMING AND CLIMATE CHANGE

Almost Gone

The great mammoths may have been threatened by disease or by a change in the climate. But many biologists believe they were hunted by the Clovis, a tribe of nomadic hunters. About 500 years ago, North America had 30 million buffalo and bison. Around 10 million of them were killed on the Great Plains in just 10 years. By the late 19th century, their numbers were in serious decline. They were killed for meat and leather, and sometimes also for sport. Today, the European bison is still endangered. If they are not protected we may lose them forever.

ECO fact

Human beings are the only animals that hunt for pleasure. All other animals kill for food or to defend themselves. Humans are also the only species that use weapons to kill.

Rarer meats are often considered a delicacy and can fetch higher prices as a result

Deserted

Life is difficult in the desert. Hunting and loss of habitat makes this life even more difficult! The goitered gazelle, for example, was the most common of all gazelle species. Today, in the deserts of Mongolia, where it once roamed, very few remain. The dama gazelle, once found in 12 countries, may soon become extinct with only 300 left in the world. The scimitar-horned oryx is already extinct.

Turning the tap off while brushing your teeth is one simple way of saving water

Where's The Water?

Three quarters of the world's surface is covered by water. Yet still there is not enough water for all our needs!

Water, Water Everywhere

We use water for domestic purposes, such as to drink and wash with, and also for industrial purposes such as generating hydroelectric energy. Water is used in religious ceremonies like baptisms and in festivals like the Thingyan water festival in Burma (Myanmar). Water is a natural resource which needs to be conserved and used sensibly.

ECO fact

In 2000, over two million people died because the rains failed and caused drought or because of diseases caused by dirty water.

GLOBAL WARMING AND CLIMATE CHANGE

Even Under The Surface

The level below the ground where water is found is called the water table. The water table is fed by the rains. Water is pumped up for homes, farms and factories. But we are pumping up more water than comes down with the rains. In 2000, the world fell short of 35 million tonnes of grain due to drought. In 2001, it was 31 million tonnes.

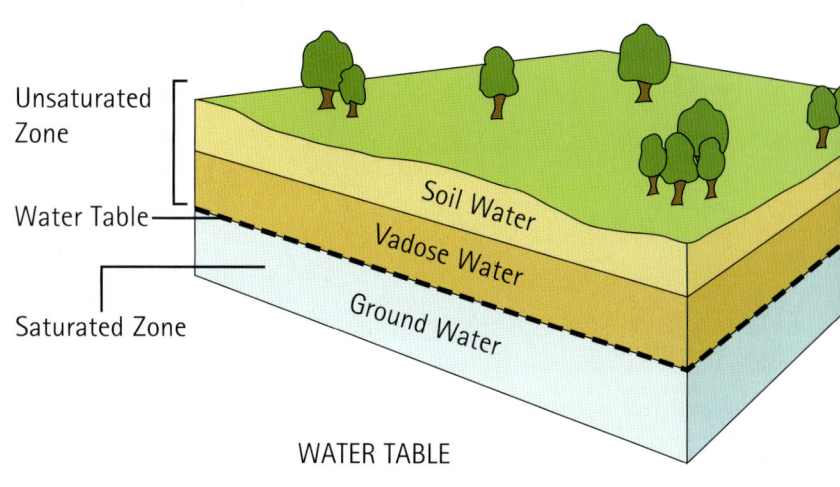

WATER TABLE

Water Riots

Water is growing so scarce that people have begun fighting over it. In some places taps are kept under lock and key. In 2000, three farmers died in a protest over giving water to the town of Jamnagar in India. In September 2007, a judge noted that almost half the murder cases from Punjab, the most prosperous farming state in India, were over water!

The increasing demand for water has led to a gross reduction in ground water in some places. This, combined with lack of rains, might soon lead to a critical lack of ground water in some places

Lack of rain in many places in Asia, Africa and Australia have led to long months of drought

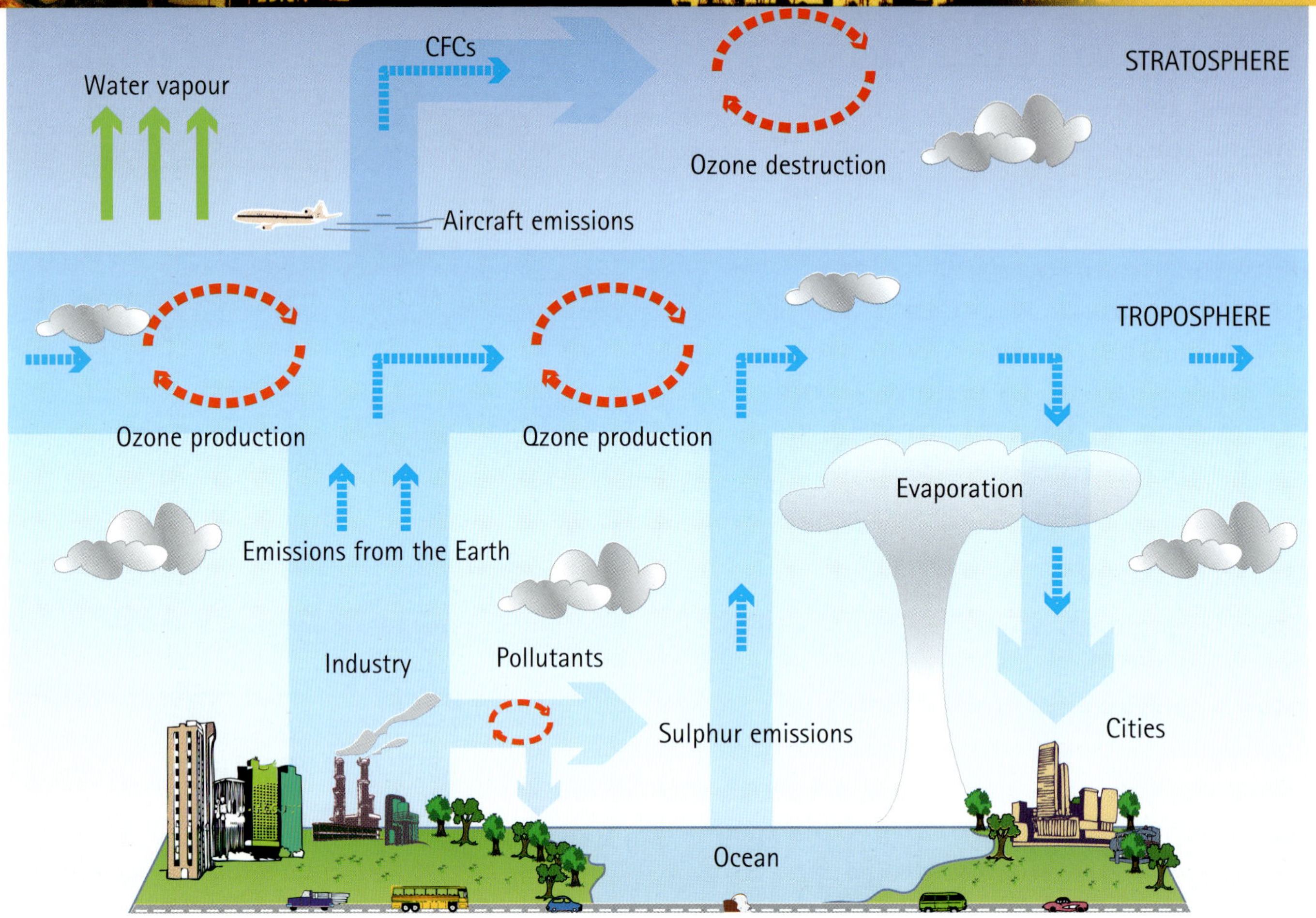

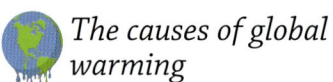

The causes of global warming

Air Pollution

Air pollution is a serious concern both in the short-term and for future generations.

Heat Can Kill

Over the last 100 years, the earth has been heating up. This is called global warming. Temperatures are predicted to rise by 1.1-6.4 degrees Centigrade (2.0-11.5 degrees Fahrenheit) by the end of this century. While volcanic eruptions can cause some of it, most of it is because of industry and other activities by humans, releasing more greenhouse gases into the atmosphere. Global warming has caused changes in the climate and the water levels in the world. It has also affected plant and animal life.

ECO fact

In December 1984, a leak from the Union Carbide factory in Bhopal, India, left more than 2,000 people dead in hours. 6,000 more died from problems caused by the gas leak.

GLOBAL WARMING AND CLIMATE CHANGE

Air pollution affects children the most, causing respiratory illnesses and other problems

Call the Doctor!

The 1990s was the hottest decade for a thousand years. Global warming may cause diseases to spread, since some germs survive better in warmer temperatures. Dangerous illnesses like yellow fever, malaria, cholera, typhoid, chikungunya, dengue are already on the rise. Schistosomiasis, lymphatic filariasis, leishmaniasis, American trypanosomiasis, or Chaga's disease, and river blindness, or onchoceriasis, may also increase.

Poison In The Air

Scientists have known about air pollution for many years. Now, it can be seen from space. At the start of this century, NASA's *Terra* spacecraft tracked air pollution around the world. The World Health Organisation estimates that 2.4 million deaths a year can be attributed to air pollution, through the development of breathing problems like bronchitis and asthma, along with heart and other lung diseases.

Excessive smoke from factories and vehicles causes smog

Burning Earth

As temperatures rise, so many parts of the earth are exposed to more extreme heat, with the many risks that that brings.

Weather Report

With summers getting hotter and longer, more people are falling ill with heat-related diseases and incidences of death from heat stroke around the world are on the rise. In 2003, about 35,000 people died in heat waves that hit Europe. With the world getting warmer, more violent storms are being recorded than ever before. Hurricanes Katrina and Rita caused massive damage. Crops that prefer cold weather like wheat, mustard, chickpea, lentil and some types of potato have less time to grow. The number of forest fires has been on the rise too. These can spread over massive areas and destroy everything in their path.

Melting Ice

The earth has about 160,000 glaciers. Almost all of them have been slowly melting away for the last century. While some of this is natural, most of it is because of human activity. They have melted the most since the mid-1990s. If glaciers continue to melt at this rate, most of them may melt away in another 50 years. Thousands of glaciers in the Himalayas are melting. The extra water is filling up mountain lakes in Nepal and Bhutan. If the water does not evaporate fast enough, the lakes will flood their banks. When this water flows down, sea levels will rise, threatening coastal regions.

Incidents of wildfires are on the increase in many countries, including the US and Australia

GLOBAL WARMING AND CLIMATE CHANGE

Goodbye To Many Things

As the world gets warmer, things we have taken for granted may be in danger. If France gets any warmer, for example, it may affect the growth of grapes and the making of wine, which will have to shift to cooler places. Pests like the pine bark beetle thrive in warm weather and attack forests of the Christmas tree pine in British Columbia. Antarctica, the white continent, has reported a new colour in winter: green, with tufts of grass showing in places they haven't been see previously.

Some scientists believe that the permanent ice layer covering the Arctic is reducing by 9 per cent every 10 years

Global warming has led to the melting of more than 13,000 sq km (5,019 sq miles) of sea ice in the Antarctic over the last 50 years

ECO fact

Since 1987, there have been increasing numbers of forest fires in the USA, burning more land than ever before. Global warming causes longer dry spells that encourage these fires.

21

Ozone Hole

The ozone is an invisible layer of the atmosphere above the earth. It protects the earth from the harmful ultraviolet (UV) rays of the sun.

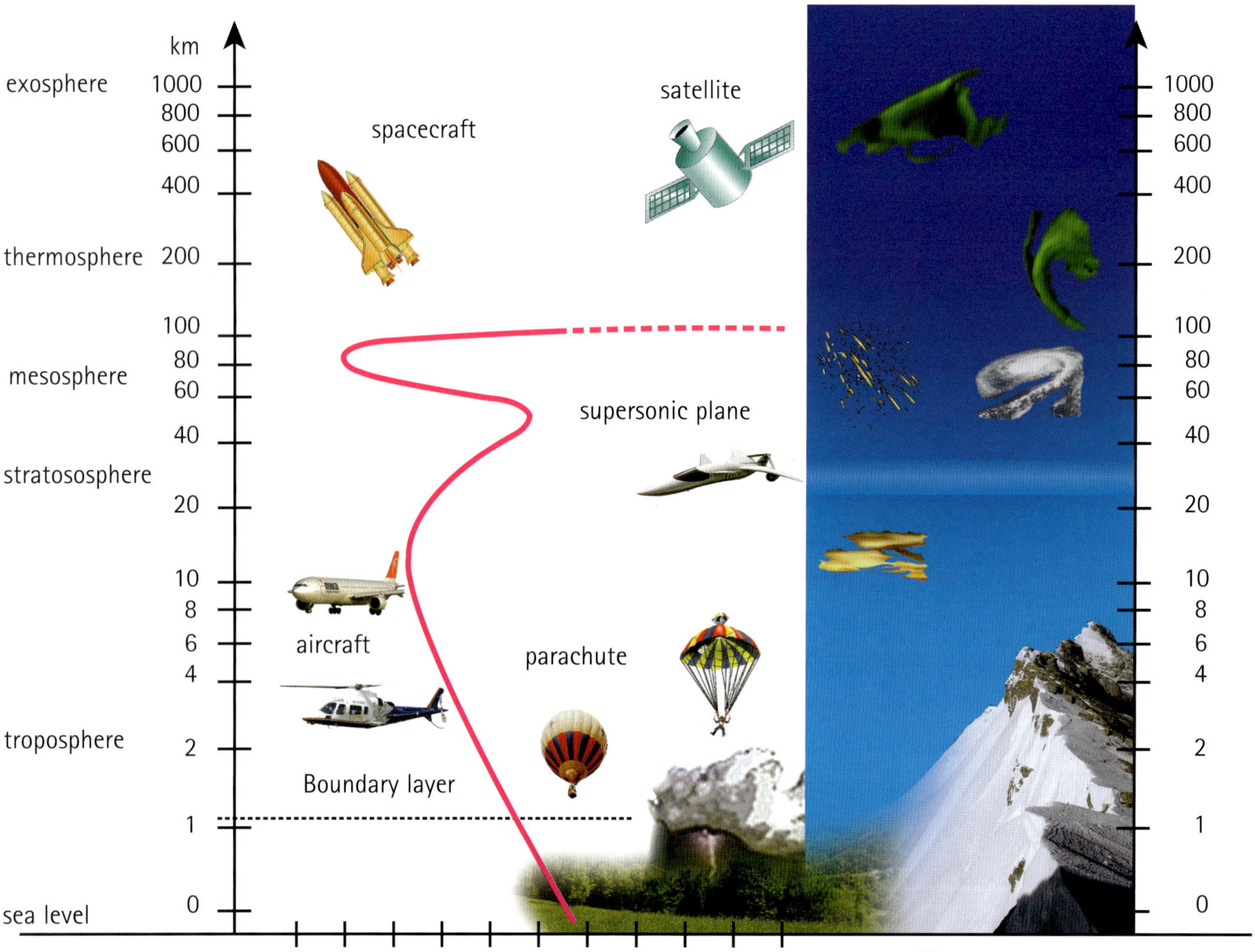

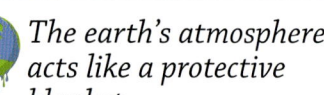

The earth's atmosphere acts like a protective blanket

More About The Blanket

In 1913, French scientists Charles Fabry and Henri Buisson discovered the ozone layer. It stretches from 15-35 km (9-21 miles) above the surface of the earth. The ozone layer is of uneven thickness; less over the equator and more at the poles. Its density is high in spring, low in autumn and increases in winter.

GLOBAL WARMING AND CLIMATE CHANGE

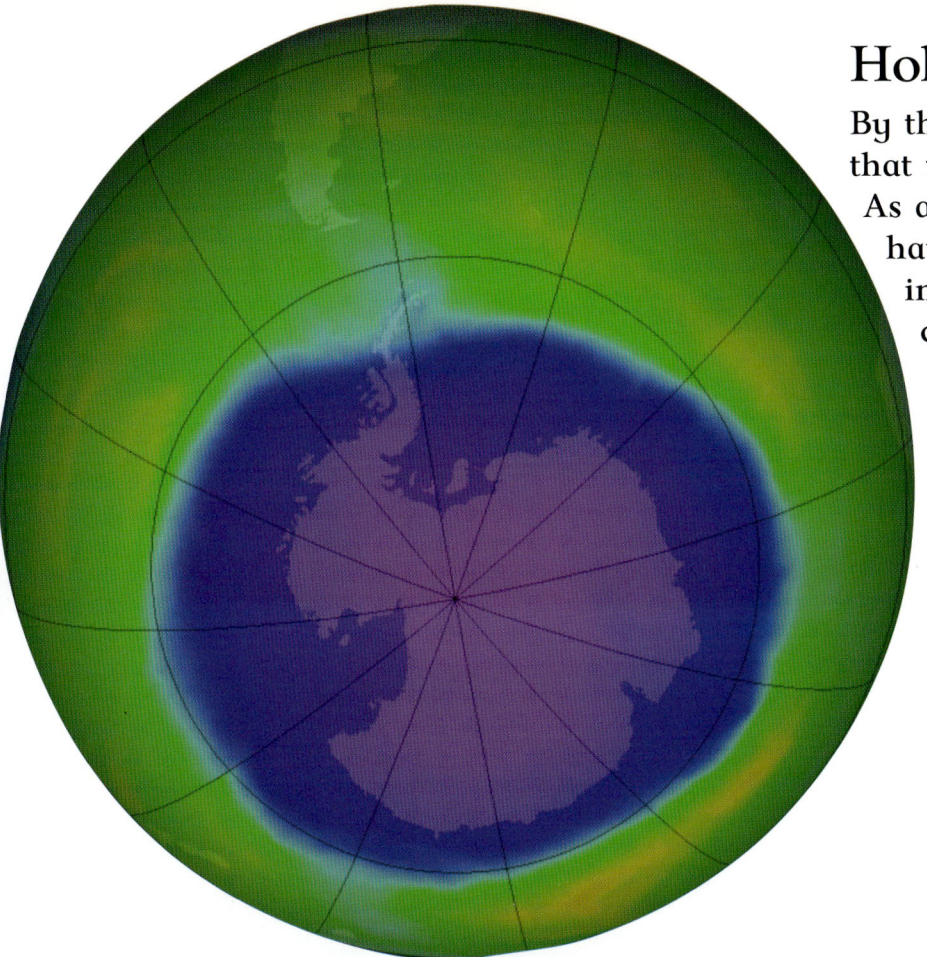

Holes In The Blanket

By the 1980s, it was well publicised that the ozone layer was decreasing. As a result certain health problems have increased, including incidences of skin cancer and cataracts.

ECO fact

British weatherman, G. M. B. Dobson, first measured the ozone layer with a spectrophotometer. The Dobson unit, used for ozone measurements, is named after him.

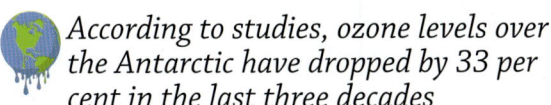
According to studies, ozone levels over the Antarctic have dropped by 33 per cent in the last three decades

Is This Also Human Made?

The thinning or depletion of the ozone layer is attributed to several factors. One of the biggest culprits is bromofluorocarbons (BFCs) and chlorofluorocarbons (CFCs), gases used in industry, in refrigerators, and to make sprays, foam and soap. CFCs rise through the atmosphere to the stratosphere, where they release chlorine. The chlorine atoms first join with ozone molecules and then break them apart. Other culprits include chemicals like methyl bromide, found in pesticides, and halons in fire extinguishers.

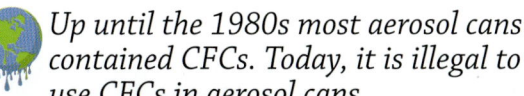
Up until the 1980s most aerosol cans contained CFCs. Today, it is illegal to use CFCs in aerosol cans

23

Rubbish Heap

Rubbish, and what to do with it, is one of the biggest challenges facing our world today. As consumers, almost everything we buy produces waste.

First Tip

Rubbish disposal has long been a problem. Archaeologists believe they have found the earliest rubbish tip, in Athens, dating from around 400 BC. By 200 BC, rubbish was becoming a real problem. So, the Romans employed the first bin men to collect rubbish! In the modern world, the English Parliament banned the dumping of waste in public places in 1388. The amount of rubbish is growing everyday and its impact upon the earth is set only to increase, unless we can find innovative ways of reducing the amount of rubbish we produce.

ECO fact

The first Earth Day was celebrated on 22 April, 1970, to make people aware of the dangers of rubbish and pollution.

GLOBAL WARMING AND CLIMATE CHANGE

How Rubbish Changes

The nature of rubbish has changed over the years. 1868 saw the first celluloid, or synthetic, plastic. Soon, plastic was being utilized, where wood, metal and bones were used previously. Other inventions that changed rubbish include cellophane (used in plastic packaging), aluminium foil, throwaway items like ballpoint pens and lighters, polyethylene-lined paper, styrofoam cups and disposable razors. By 1963, drinks cans had made their way on to shop shelves.

Recyclable waste ends up in a recycling centre where it is processed into raw materials to be used again

Rubbish is most commonly buried in landfills

The Three Rs

The three Rs aim to reduce rubbish. Remember: reduce, reuse and recycle. If each of us reduces the amount of stuff we throw out, it makes a huge difference. There are many things we can reuse, such as plastic bags. More rubbish than you might think can be recycled.

Rubbish should be divided into biodegradable, recyclable and non-recyclable waste

Red Alert

Waste can be harmful to our health. Toxic or dangerous waste is mainly made up of chemicals that can poison living things, including trees, insects and animals.

From All Over

Toxic waste has been increasing since the Industrial Revolution. Most toxic waste comes from factories, hospitals and agriculture. These sources can release chemicals into water, land and the air. Toxic wastes include mercury, lead, asbestos and acid from batteries. They can cause birth defects, illnesses like cancer and may kill many people and animals.

Over the last couple of decades diseases like cancer and respiratory diseases have been on the rise

ECO fact

Nuclear waste includes plutonium, uranium and other radioactive elements. Most of them emit large amounts of radiation. They can stay active for as long as 100,000 years.

GLOBAL WARMING AND CLIMATE CHANGE

Toxic Trade

Believe it or not, toxic waste is actually traded! Industries in developed countries sell toxic waste to countries that often have less stringent regulations about how it is processed. For years, shiploads of toxic waste have been sent to Papua New Guinea, the Philippines, India and Russia to be recycled.

 *Toxic waste from factories can pollute the air and water*

Can The Waste Be Treated?

Toxic waste can be treated. However, it is expensive and a matter of international debate. In 1989, about 50 countries signed The Basel Convention on the Control of Transboundary Movement of Hazardous Wastes and their Disposal, a treaty to regulate dumping toxic waste. Toxic waste can also be produced by hospitals that treat diseases like cancer with radiation therapy. This kind of waste needs to be isolated and disposed of carefully. Nuclear waste is the result of nuclear fission. A large amount of nuclear waste stored under Lake Karachay in Russia has been dispersed by storms as the lake has dried up over the years. Indeed, the lake is said to be the most polluted place on the planet!

Most countries have strict laws about disposal of toxic waste

Wild Weather

Global warming causes temperatures to rise fractionally, but this small change can bring about marked changes to the climate. Some of these changes are hardly noticeable, others dramatic.

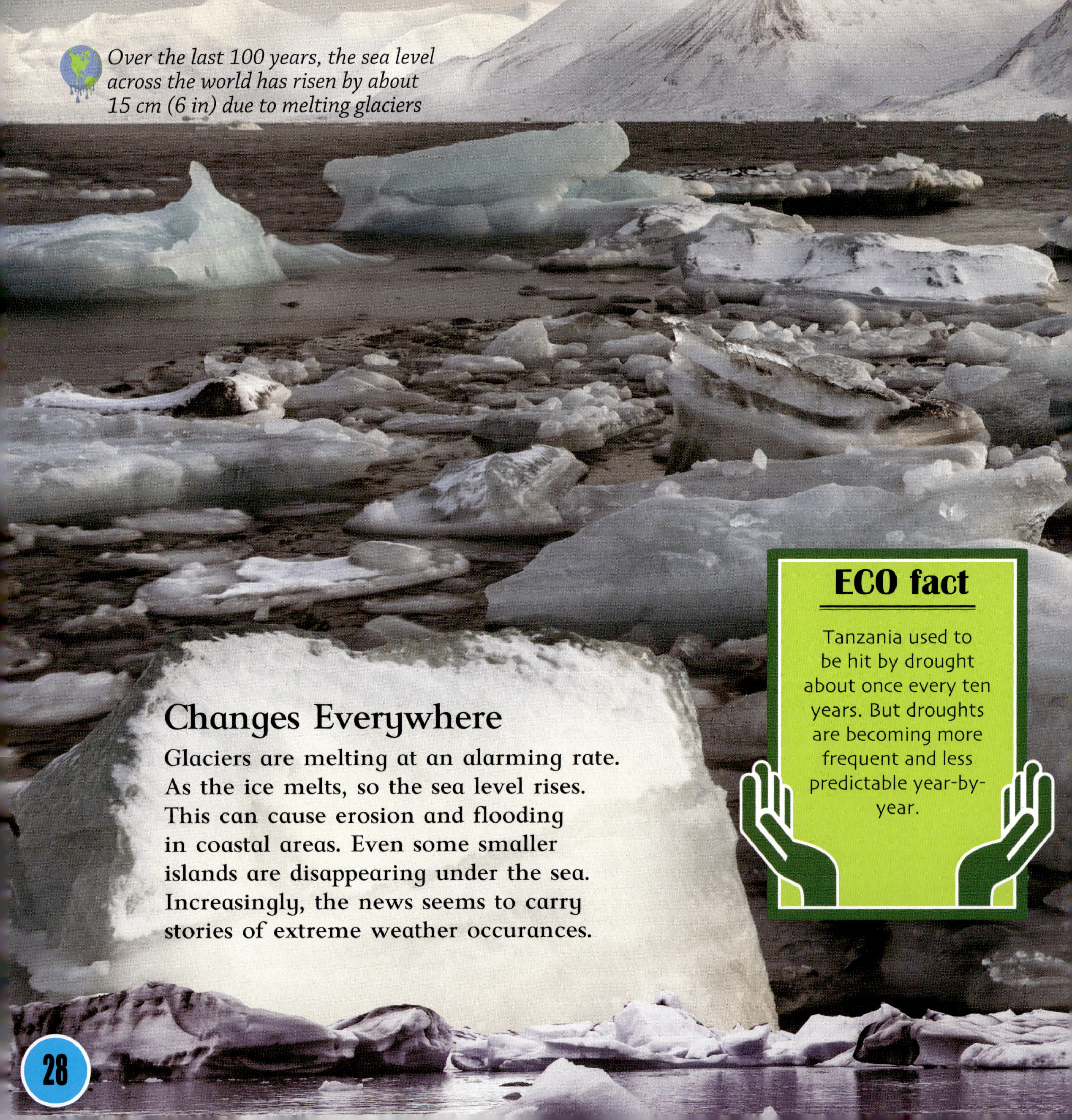

Over the last 100 years, the sea level across the world has risen by about 15 cm (6 in) due to melting glaciers

Changes Everywhere

Glaciers are melting at an alarming rate. As the ice melts, so the sea level rises. This can cause erosion and flooding in coastal areas. Even some smaller islands are disappearing under the sea. Increasingly, the news seems to carry stories of extreme weather occurances.

ECO fact

Tanzania used to be hit by drought about once every ten years. But droughts are becoming more frequent and less predictable year-by-year.

GLOBAL WARMING AND CLIMATE CHANGE

Raining Buckets

Rain patterns around the world are changing, becoming increasingly unpredictable. As the world becomes warmer, the clash of hot and cold air between low and high pressure areas increases. This causes violent hurricanes and storms. The number of hurricanes touching wind speeds of 56 metres per second increased by 15 per cent between the 1970s and 1990s!

Melting permafrost contributes to global warming by releasing methane

Permanent No More

Icy tundra regions are known for permafrost - a layer of soil that remains frozen throughout the year. This permafrost absorbs carbon from the air. As global temperatures have risen, this permafrost has begun to melt. As this happens the carbon dioxide and methane that was 'locked-in' is released.

Violent hurricanes like Hurricane Katrina are becoming more frequent

Rising Sea Levels

The period 1650 to 1850 has become known as the Little Ice Age. In the years that have followed the world has become warmer, partly as a result of human behaviour it is believed. As a result, glaciers and other ice bodies are melting faster than before.

The Himalayan glaciers are retreating at an alarming rate

Less Ice Everywhere

The 1990s was the hottest decade in the last thousand years and glaciers all over the world have been melting faster since then. Gigantic mountain ranges like the Himalayas, the Rocky Mountains of America and the Alps of Europe are losing some of their ice caps. Glaciers in the Himalayas in India have been retreating by up to 15 m (50 ft) every year in some parts. Water from glaciers feeds rivers and give us water to drink and use. But if the ice melts too quickly, the world faces a potentially catastrophic water shortage.

ECO fact

The US Geological Survey and NASA are working together on Glims (Global Land Ice Measurements from Space), a satellite project that measures the melting of glaciers.

GLOBAL WARMING AND CLIMATE CHANGE

Flooded Away

As glaciers melt, the water fills lakes and rivers. Dozens of lakes in the Himalayas are holding so much water that they are liable to burst their banks, which could cause devastating flooding. By 2050, most of the glaciers in several mountain ranges, including the Rockies, may have melted away. Qori Kalis, a glacier in the Andes in Peru, South America, is losing as much ice in a week as it used to in a year!

Down To The Sea

The water from melting glaciers finally arrives at sea level. Since 1900, sea levels have been rising about 2 mm (0.08 in) every year. Since 1993, they have risen about 3.1 mm (0.12 in) a year. That means a rise of 15-30 cm (6-12 in) in 100 years. This rise is also caused by sea water expanding as the oceans become warmer. More water leads to more floods along coastal areas. Low-lying regions and islands are being eroded and people, animals and plants are under threat.

Coastal flooding and storm surges are on the rise

The level of water in seas and oceans is rising every year. As a result flooding in coastal regions are becoming more common

31

Food Shortage

Temperature affects all life on earth. The world is getting hotter because of global warming. It is also becoming more crowded. There is increasing fear of severe food shortages.

Crops Cropped

Farmland in many regions is being reduced in size for many reasons. There are more people today than ever before. They need space to live in, to study and work in. Millions of acres of farmland are being made into roads, rail tracks and new suburbs. In parts of the developed world people buy more food than they need and often throw much of it away. Britain, for example, throws away about a third of the food it buys. People who can afford it often eat more than they need, while others suffer from starvation.

Not Enough Water

Global warming has changed the weather conditions in many parts of the world. In 2007, Australia faced a terrible drought followed by floods. Indeed, droughts have plagued parts of Australia for five consecutive years. With water drying up in these regions, farmers have been selling their cattle cheaply before they die of thirst and hunger. It is the underdeveloped and developing countries that suffer the most from these natural disasters. Farmers are leaving agriculture and turning to other work.

Droughts are leading to the drying-up of arable lands. Better irrigation systems are thus required to produce crops more efficiently

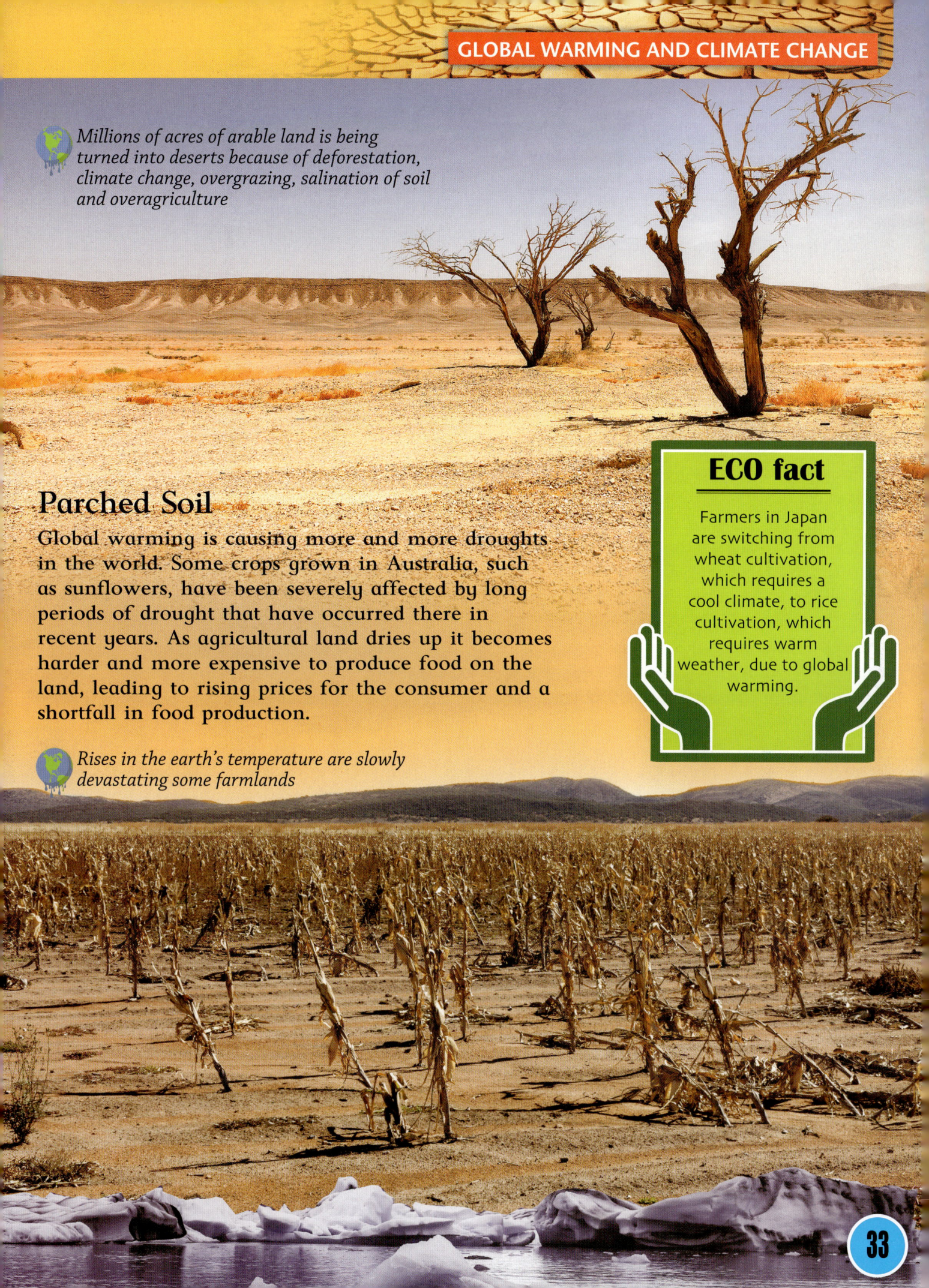

GLOBAL WARMING AND CLIMATE CHANGE

Millions of acres of arable land is being turned into deserts because of deforestation, climate change, overgrazing, salination of soil and overagriculture

Parched Soil

Global warming is causing more and more droughts in the world. Some crops grown in Australia, such as sunflowers, have been severely affected by long periods of drought that have occurred there in recent years. As agricultural land dries up it becomes harder and more expensive to produce food on the land, leading to rising prices for the consumer and a shortfall in food production.

Rises in the earth's temperature are slowly devastating some farmlands

ECO fact

Farmers in Japan are switching from wheat cultivation, which requires a cool climate, to rice cultivation, which requires warm weather, due to global warming.

At the Poles

About 125 lakes have dried up in the Arctic regions in less than half a century. These lakes were fed by the permafrost, or the layer below the ground, that used to be frozen all the time. This permafrost has begun melting and evaporating because of global warming.

Not Jumping For Joy

Temperatures have been rising in the Canadian Arctic region for the past 50 years. As temperatures rise life becomes increasingly difficult for the animals of the region. As ice melts polar bears find it increasingly difficult to hunt. Polar bears are strong swimmers and can cross large stretches of water at a time. But less food makes them weaker and swimming harder. As a result, polar bears are increasingly under threat.

A polar bear stands on a piece of floating ice. The rise in the Arctic temperatures is causing sea ice to melt faster

Is Their Fate Sealed?

As the Polar waters get warmer seals find it more difficult to find the food they are used to eating. They feed on krill, plankton and algae, all of which need cool waters to live. With less to eat adult seals are thinner and so their babies are weaker and their numbers are falling. The population of a colony of elephant seals in the Southern Ocean dropped by half between the 1950s and 1985.

Seals are dying due to excessive heat and the shortage of food

GLOBAL WARMING AND CLIMATE CHANGE

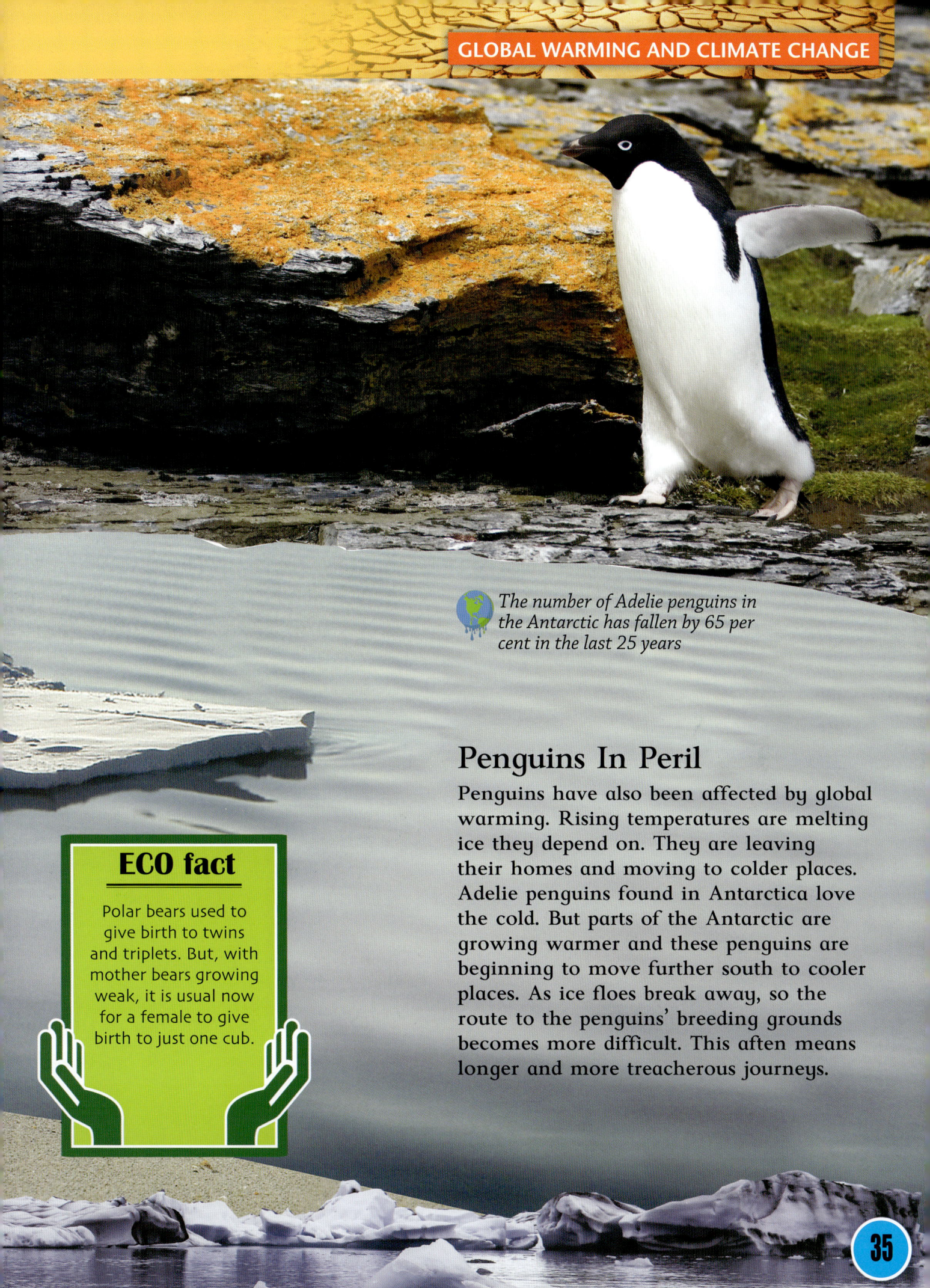

The number of Adelie penguins in the Antarctic has fallen by 65 per cent in the last 25 years

Penguins In Peril

Penguins have also been affected by global warming. Rising temperatures are melting ice they depend on. They are leaving their homes and moving to colder places. Adelie penguins found in Antarctica love the cold. But parts of the Antarctic are growing warmer and these penguins are beginning to move further south to cooler places. As ice floes break away, so the route to the penguins' breeding grounds becomes more difficult. This aften means longer and more treacherous journeys.

ECO fact

Polar bears used to give birth to twins and triplets. But, with mother bears growing weak, it is usual now for a female to give birth to just one cub.

Change No Good

Some birds and animals migrate to warmer places in winter. However, global warming is beginning to affect some migratory patterns.

Large areas of grassland are destroyed by forest fires each year

New Visitors

Animals and birds are trying to adapt to a warmer world and in some cases this is changing migratory patterns. The UK, for example, is seeing some new visitors. Birds like the little egret and water creatures like the loggerhead turtle are swimming north to enjoy the cooler British climate. Even fish like the red mullet are becoming common in the seas around Britain. The ringed plover, a wading bird, has shifted from the west coast to the east coast in Britain. But not all animals can adapt. The flying fox of Australia, for example, is reducing in number as its migratory habitat changes.

Animals on the Move

Global warming has affected the migratory patterns of animals as well. The savannah grasslands of Africa are beginning to disappear. One of the reasons for this is forest fires. As a result many grazing animals such as zebras and wildebeest are moving out of places like the Kruger National Park in South Africa and plant-eating animals like elephants and leopards can be seen in places they were not found before.

The migratory routes of many animals are changing

GLOBAL WARMING AND CLIMATE CHANGE

Fight To The Finish?

Some birds are changing their migration routes as well. The European blackcap would previously breed in Germany in the summer and fly south-west to Spain in winter. But now, some of them migrate west to England during the winter months. The migration back to Germany becomes faster for these 'English' blackcaps meaning they often occupy the best nesting places. As a result, the birds that still fly to Spain may soon be forced to change their winter home or die out. It is believed that the migratory pattern of the hummingbird may also be affected by global warming. They are now found in places they were not found before.

The migratory patterns of some hummingbirds has changed due to global warming

ECO fact

The red fox finds it difficult to adapt to warmer weather and is moving north to the Arctic regions. This potentially threatens the Arctic fox as the red fox is a predator.

Human World

Human beings not only cause global warming, but are also its biggest victims.

Changing World
Climate affects almost everything we do. Our food, water and even the air we breathe is changing because of global warming.

ECO fact
Despite all the advances in science and technology increasing the production of crops, still millions of people go hungry in the world.

Snow storms are being seen in places they were not seen before

GLOBAL WARMING AND CLIMATE CHANGE

Hurricane Katrina caused large scale damage in New Orleans in 2005

Stormy Weather

Scientists who study weather believe that global warming is causing more violent storms than ever before. Researchers from Purdue University say that parts of the USA may have more severe storms in the coming years. About 160,000 people, most of whom are poor children, in Africa, Asia, and South America, have died in recent years because of extreme weather and the spread of diseases caused by climate change.

Dry Land

The average temperature of the earth is rising. The pattern of rainfall is shifting towards the Poles and away from hot Equatorial regions where it is desperately needed for the production of crops. This is slowly forcing millions of people from their homes as they can't produce enough food to survive. Population displacement has a knock-on effect that increases the pressure on the production of food elsewhere.

Spread of Diseases

Our health is also affected by the climate. Warm weather and flooding in particular can help breed and carry diseases that would not otherwise have spread.

Blowing Hot

In August 2003, Europe faced a terrible heat wave. Thousands of people fell severely ill. About 35,000 mostly old and sick people died around Europe as a direct result. People were not prepared for such high temperatures and did not know how to keep themselves safe from the heat. the elderly are most at risk if the temperature rises too much.

Fly By Night And Day

Several germs and insects that spread disease breed in warm weather. Mosquitoes spread illnesses that can cause people to die. These include malaria, chikungunya, yellow fever and dengue. Bacteria like salmonella, which cause paratyphoid and typhoid, thrive in warm weather. Highly infectious diseases like cholera can also spread. Warm weather encourages the growth of insects like the house fly which spreads dysentery, cholera, typhoid and anthrax. These disease-causing germs and insects are active during both day and night.

Children playing in a public fountain to beat the heat

GLOBAL WARMING AND CLIMATE CHANGE

Hot Under The Skin

A thinning ozone layer and the hole in the ozone blanket exposes us to more harmful ultra violet rays from the sun. This has increased incidences of skin cancer. Doctors fear that the change in climate may lead to 5,000 more people dying from skin cancer every year. It is therefore important to be aware of the precautions you should take from the sun: avoid prolonged exposure to direct sunlight; wear a high-factor sun screen and cover up with a hat and suitable clothing.

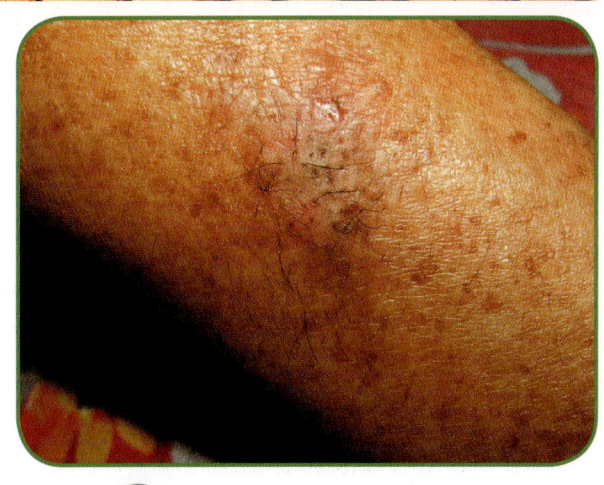

The harmful rays from the sun have increased diseases like skin cancer

ECO fact

Harmful ultra violet rays are a danger to people's eyesight. In the UK, this is expected to cause an extra 2,000 cases of cataracts.

An emergency worker gives a vaccine in a flood-affected area. Water-borne diseases are a danger during floods

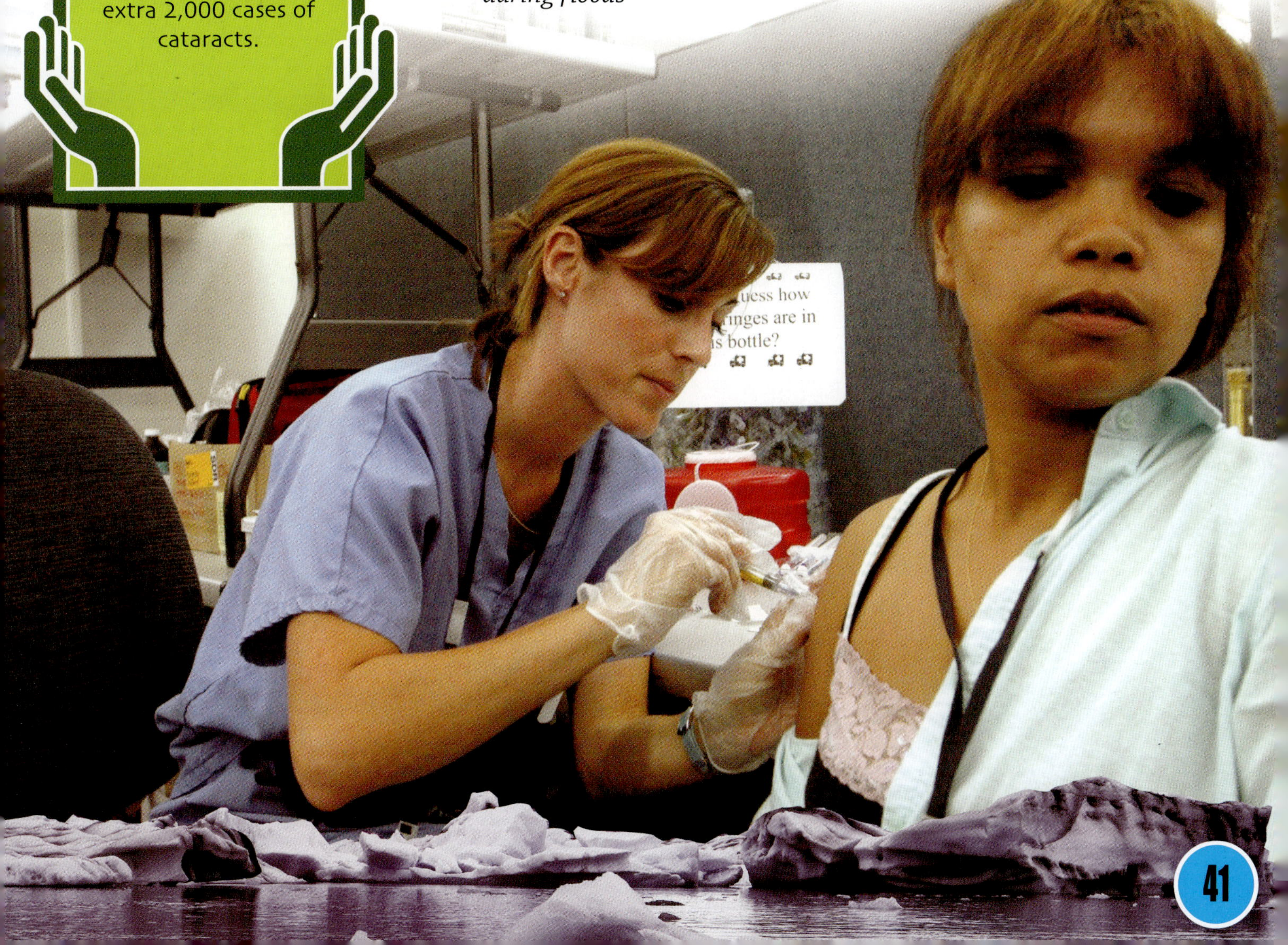

Can We Stop It?

Global warming is an issue which needs to be taken up by governments, big and small industries, as well as ordinary citizens.

World Organisations

Several organisations work in various countries for a healthier environment. One of the largest is UNEP, or the United Nations Environment Programme, set up in 1972 after the UN Conference on the Human Environment. The World Wide Fund for Nature was set up in 1961. It works in more than 100 countries, funding about 2,000 conservation projects across the world. Another landmark in the fight against global warming was the Rio Declaration (1992), which laid down certain basic priciples for the fight against global warming. The Kyoto Protocol, held in Japan (1997), spoke about the need to reduce greenhouse gases.

Many countries now have strict laws to control pollution

ECO fact

The Montreal Protocol works to reduce the use of products that damage the ozone layer. It came into effect on 1 January 1989 and has 191 member countries.

GLOBAL WARMING AND CLIMATE CHANGE

Industries

One of the greatest contributors to greenhouse gas emmissions are factories. Big and small industries can do a lot to reduce the harmful effects of greenhouse gases. Filters can be placed in factory chimneys which prevent dangerous gases from escaping into the air. Cleaner and safer energy can be used to power the factories. Money can be invested by the industrial sector into research on safer energy sources.

Waste treatment plants like this one help reduce the amount of waste let out by factories

The Populace

We as a society can perhaps make the most difference. More trees can be planted. Emissions from vehicles could be greatly reduced if people walked or cycled more. Energy saving in the home and recycling can also have a big effect.

Car manufacturers are now making cars that run on alternative fuels like hydrogen

43

You Can Help Too

Get Growing!

Ask your parents or school if you can plant a tree. Try to grow the tree from the seed of a local fruit you have eaten. A tree that grows in that climate will grow faster and healthier than one that is used to a different climate. It would be difficult for a mango tree to grow where conifers thrive!

⊘ Here's How:
- The best time for this is in spring.
- Ask your parents if you may use an old take-away tub.
- Request help to make a hole at the bottom from which extra water can drain out.
- Cover the hole with small bits of brick or pieces from a broken terracotta pot.
- Fill with equal parts of earth, dry leaves and sand, leaving an inch at the top.
- Plant the seed.
- Sprinkle some water. Keep it in a cool, dark place.
- When the shoot appears, shift it to more light.
- Water regularly. Look after it through winter. The next spring, plant it in the spot you have chosen and watch it grow!

⊘ Green Up The Globe
- Check with your parents whether they recycle household waste. Many councils collect recyling from your home, so it's easy to do!
- Why not compost the food waste from your kitchen? It's great for the worms and good for your garden!
- Try to cut down on the amount of packaging you use.

GLOBAL WARMING AND CLIMATE CHANGE

Shop Green

- Try to cut down on waste by thinking more about what you're buying and whether you really need it. Writing a shopping is a good idea. You could also save some money!
- Try not to shop every day. Make a weekly list, even for things like stationery and sweets. The less you shop, the less you waste!

Save Energy

- Ask your parents whether the light bulbs they use are energy saving or not. Energy saving light bulbs use a lot less energy than regular light bulbs and they last a lot longer too!
- Switch off the lights every time you leave an empty room.
- If you use an immersion heater to heat water, use it sparingly and only when needed.

Try to re-use the bags you get with your shopping

Ensure that you use energy saving bulbs at home

Planting trees is a fun way of helping the environment!

45